Christmas Time
It's All About Jesus!

Written by Sue M. Barksdale

Illustrated by Alicia T. Young

It's Christmas time and what do you see?

Santas and reindeer and Christmas trees.

Stockings and bows and presents galore;

But Christmas is so much, Oh SO much MORE!

It's all about
JESUS,
how to **this** world He came,
And ever since then,
It's not been
the same!

For you see
He was born
a BABY
for GLORY,
It's a wonderful,
awesome,
AMAZING
story!

Let's start with the angel who came to bring
Good news that Mary
would soon have the KING.

Mary was troubled
and just couldn't see
ANY
possible
way
this could
come
to be!

Gently the angel said,
"Don't be afraid!"
By God's Spirit
this child will be made."

"I am the Lord's servant,"
Mary did say.
Hearing her words,
the angel
went on his way.

So Mary hurried to Judah, her cousin to see;
The greeting was special, just what could it be?

'Twas Elizabeth's baby leaping in her with joy
For Mary was carrying
THE special boy!

Now Mary was engaged to Joseph,
A man who had a big part in God's
greatest
plan.

Like Mary,
Joseph was somewhat afraid,
But God sent an angel to help the fear fade.

"Don't be afraid," Joseph heard in a dream, and what was said next made his heart beam.

"A Son will be born," the angel repeated, With news about Jesus, the dream was completed.

Up from his sleep,
Joe made Mary his bride,
Then they set out
together
to take a long ride.

Mary was ready
as on a donkey she mounted,
For the Romans had said
everyone must be counted.

Each man must return
to the place he was born,
Thus setting the scene for the first Christmas morn.

Called the city of David,
Bethlehem
was its name.
With many others,
to this city
they came.

The time had now come for Jesus' birth,
And so as a baby He came to this Earth.
Having no crib, Mary did what she could,

She swaddled
and lay him,
in a manger of wood.

What happened next
should be no surprise,
to some shepherd guys.

An angel appeared

what the angel did say,

Now you can guess

"Don't be afraid,"

was the message he gave.

"A Savior is born!" was the news he was bringing.
As an angel host joined him, with praises and singing
"Glory to God in the highest and peace on Earth!"
Then returning to heaven, they rejoiced at this birth.

Quickly the shepherds hurried to find
The babe in the manger - there was the sign!

After they saw, they went spreading the word,
And all were amazed
at the message they heard.

Treasuring up all these things in her heart,
Mary pondered this birth
and its special part

Of the story
of LIFE
through God's
only Son,
Bringing news
of great JOY
for everyone!

So cattle and shepherds
and a sweet girl named Mary,
and angels with news
of the child she would
carry,

Make
the Christmas season
a wonderful time
To celebrate the happenings
told in this rhyme.

And when we do like Mary and treasure in our hearts
Jesus and His story – the most important part
We'll find that bows on presents and Christmas trees are fun–

Happy Birthday JESUS!

But the greatest CELEBRATION is the birthday of GOD'S Son!

Christmas Time

Christmas Time Devotions

On the second page of this book, it says,
"Jesus was born as a baby for glory!"
What does that mean?
The word glory means magnificence and praiseworthy.
Jesus' birth was no ordinary birth because
Jesus is no ordinary man!
He is God, and His birth was for a very special purpose.

On the next few pages, you will find five short devotions
using the letters in the word glory.
It is our prayer that these, along with
Christmas Time - It's All About Jesus!
will help you celebrate Jesus at Christmas and throughout the year!

John 1:14, "The Word became flesh and took up residence among us.
We observed His glory, the glory as the One and Only Son
from the Father, full of grace and truth."

Jesus Came as a Gift

Why do we give gifts? Why do we spend time making or buying special things for our family and friends at Christmas? When someone gives you a gift, how does that make you feel?

God gave us the most special gift we could ever receive when He sent Jesus to earth as a baby. The Bible says in John 3:16, "For God so loved the world that He gave His only Son." On that first Christmas morning, Jesus was born as God's gift to the world. God gave Jesus because He loves us so much and wants us to know Him.

Father,
Thank You for Your love for us. Thank you for sending Your Son, Jesus, as the most special gift. During this Christmas season as I see gifts given and received, I will remember Your gift of Love.
In Jesus' Name,
Amen.

Family Activities

Talk about what kind of gifts you can give this Christmas that will make other people feel loved. What are some gifts you can give that will "keep on giving?" One idea is to make a calendar for the coming year with hand-drawn illustrations and hand-written Scriptures.

Jesus Came as the Light

Why do we need light? To help us see when it's dark, right?
Have you ever been in the dark? What does that feel like?
Then what do you feel like when someone turns the light on?
Have you ever been outside at nighttime?
When it's dark, you need some light to show you the way home. The Bible says that people are lost in the darkness and need light. Jesus came to be the light that shows us the way home. He said, "I have come as a light into the world, so that everyone who believes in Me would not remain in darkness" (John 12:46)

Father,
Thank you for sending Jesus to be our Light.
We couldn't make it home without Him. This Christmas, as I look at all the Christmas lights, I will be reminded that Jesus is the best light of all!
In Jesus' Name,
Amen.

Family Activities
Talk with your family about how you can brighten the world around you during this Christmas season. One idea is to decorate a mini-tree with lights or wrap up some pretty candles and deliver them to an elderly neighbor.
Add a note telling them that
the Light of the world has come!

Jesus Came as the Only Door

We don't think much about doors. They don't seem very exciting, do they?
But what if we didn't have them? Talk with your family about the purposes
of doors. To go in, to go out, to keep loved ones protected, to keep critters out -
there are many reasons why doors are important.
What if there was no door to your room? There would be no way to get in, right?
What if you arrived at a new school and you couldn't find the door
to go inside? How would you feel? Would you be glad when someone
showed you the way? Jesus talked about being the way to God.
He said, "I am the Door. If anyone enters by Me, he will be saved,
and will come in and go out and find pasture" (John 10:9).

Father,
Thank you for sending Jesus to be the Door to your kingdom.
And thank you that we are invited in! As I look at festively decorated doors
this Christmas season, I will remember that You are the Only Door!
In Jesus' Name,
Amen.

Family Activities

Many people decorate their doors with pretty wreaths and lights
at Christmas time. Think about how you could decorate
your door to make it show the true meaning of the season
to all who enter - and even to all who pass by!
Another idea is to make some homemade wreaths to give to
friends and family and pray for opportunities
to share that Jesus is the Door to heaven.

Jesus Came so we can Rejoice in Him

What does it mean to be joyful or to have joy? Joy is almost the same thing
as happiness. To be joyful is to be glad about something. The Bible says
that Jesus is the source of true joy, and we feel that joy when we are glad in Him.
Over 700 years before Jesus came to earth, God told the great prophet Isaiah
that He would send someone who would bring great joy to everyone
who needed it : "Shout aloud and sing for joy, people of Zion, for great
is the Holy One of Israel among you" (Isaiah 12:6). That someone was Jesus.
Think for a moment about what makes you happy and what makes you sad.
Most of the time what makes us happy or sad are things that don't last very long.
Opening Christmas gifts can make us happy, but after a while, the gift
doesn't give us the joy it used to. But being glad in Jesus is something that
can give us joy all the time - and forever!

Father,
Thank you for sending Jesus to give us joy! Help me to be more glad about Jesus
than anything else, or anyone else, so that my joy is always with me.
In Jesus' Name,
Amen.

Family Activities
One way to rejoice in God is to sing praise songs together as a family.
One possibility to share your joy is an old-fashioned caroling through
the neighborhood, singing some familiar Christmas carols. You may want to
carry some candy canes along to hand out to your neighbors.
(Do an online search for "The history of the candy cane" for an added note.)

Jesus Came as the Yes to God's Promises

What is a promise? A promise is stating very surely
that you will or will not do something. Have you ever made a promise to someone,
maybe your best friend or a family member?
Was it easy to keep that promise? Has someone made you a promise
and maybe didn't keep it? How did that make you feel?
The Bible is filled with promises from God, and it says, "For every one of
God's promises is "Yes" in Him." (2 Cor. 1:20). He has promised that He will never leave us,
that He has good plans for our lives, that we can do all things through His strength -
all these and so many more - because Jesus came!
How is Christmas a promise from God? The Bible says in Isaiah 7:14
that the Messiah, Jesus, would be born.
God kept His promise on that first Christmas morning!

Father,
Thank You for always keeping Your promises and that they are all "Yes"
because of Jesus. Help me to trust You. I love you.
In Jesus' Name,
Amen.

Family Activities
As a family, do an online search for God's promises and
have each family member pick out a favorite.
One way to remember that promise from year to year
is to make an ornament out of whatever materials you have handy.
Write your promise, name, and date on it, and hang it on the tree or in your room.
Watch to see how God answers "yes"
to that promise in the coming year.

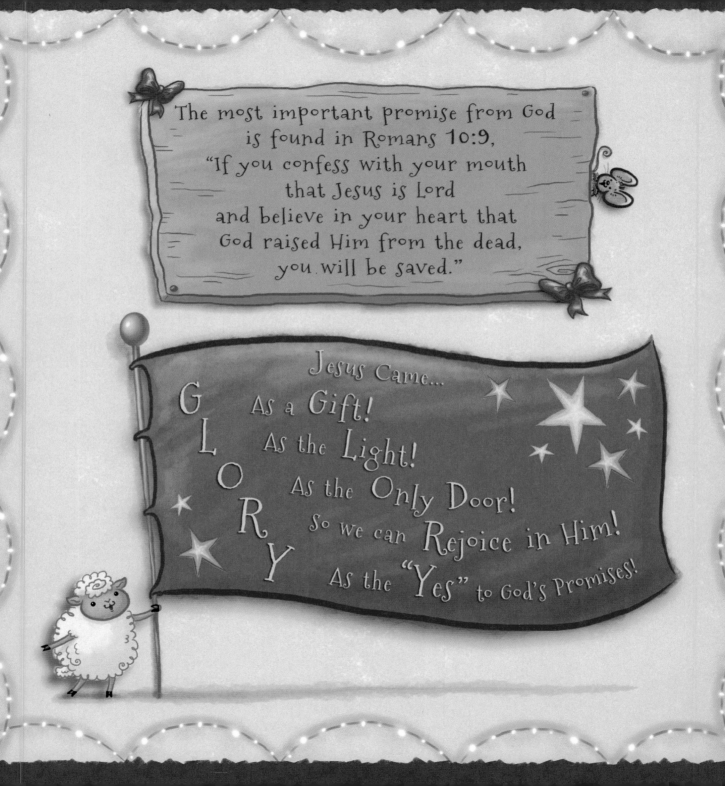

The most important promise from God
is found in Romans 10:9,
"If you confess with your mouth
that Jesus is Lord
and believe in your heart that
God raised Him from the dead,
you will be saved."

Jesus Came...

G As a Gift!

L As the Light!

O As the Only Door!

R So we can Rejoice in Him!

Y As the "Yes" to God's Promises!

Also by the Author

Available where books are sold

While there are many activities and voices vying for your children's time and attention, there are few that are more important than you teaching your children to pray. Cultivating a vibrant relationship with their Creator is the key that opens the door for your children to have a fulfilling and purposeful life.

In this book you will find a creative, delightful tool to use as you help your children learn to pray. They will enjoy the beautiful illustrations and thoughtful, rhyming text. You will appreciate the way the pattern for prayer is laid out in an easy-to-remember format. And together you will open the G.I.F.T.S. of prayer and find the One "who is able to do exceedingly, abundantly above all we ask or can even imagine."

Christmas Time – Sue M. Barksdale

Copyright © 2015

First edition published 2015

All rights reserved. No part of this book may be reproduced, stored in a retrieval system, or transmitted in any form or by any means – electronic, mechanical, photocopying, recording, or otherwise, without written permission from the publisher.

Unless otherwise noted, Bible verses are from the Holman Christian Standard Bible® Copyright © 1999, 2000, 2002, 2003, 2009, by Holman Bible Publishers. Used with permission.

Scripture quotations marked (NIV) are taken from the Holy Bible, New International Version®, NIV®. Copyright © 1973, 1978, 1984, 2011 by Biblica, Inc.™ Used by permission of Zondervan. All rights reserved worldwide. www.zondervan.com The "NIV" and "New International Version" are trademarks registered in the United States Patent and Trademark Office by Biblica, Inc.™

Illustrator: Alicia R. Young

Editor: Sheila Wilkinson

Printed in the United States of America

Aneko Press – *Our Readers Matter*™

www.anekopress.com

Aneko Press, Life Sentence Publishing, and our logos are trademarks of

Life Sentence Publishing, Inc.
203 E. Birch Street
P.O. Box 652
Abbotsford, WI 54405

**JUVENILE NONFICTION /
Holidays & Celebrations /
Christmas & Advent**

Paperback ISBN: 978-1-62245-249-1

eBook ISBN: 978-1-62245-250-7

10 9 8 7 6 5 4 3 2

Available where books are sold

Made in the USA
Middletown, DE
10 December 2021